A Bustle & Sew Publication

Copyright © Bustle & Sew Limited 2013

The right of Helen Dickson to be identified as the author of this work has been asserted in accordance with the Copyright, Designs and Patents Act 1988.

All rights reserved. No part of this publication may be reproduced, stored in a retrieval system or transmitted in any form, or by any means, without the prior written permission of the author, nor be otherwise circulated in any form of binding or cover other than that in which it is published and without a similar condition being imposed on the subsequent purchaser.

Every effort has been made to ensure that all the information in this book is accurate. However, due to differing conditions, tools and individual skills, the publisher cannot be responsible for any injuries, losses and other damages that may result from the use of the information in this book.

ISBN-13: 978-1495355165

ISBN-10: 1495355160

First published 2014 by:
Bustle & Sew
Coombe Leigh
Chillington
Kingsbridge
Devon TQ7 2LE
UK

www.bustleandsew.com

Hello, and welcome to the February 2014 issue of the Bustle & Sew Magazine. There's lots to enjoy in this month's issue, including the return of Bear who posed for my Little Cupid Bear design on page 5. I've also started a new series of articles which I hope will be interesting and helpful to those of you who enjoy making to sell, whether for profit or for a charitable cause. You'll also discover lots of bunnies to make in plenty of time for Easter.

Notes from a Devon Village is taking a bit of a break - I love to write about life here in Devon in my blog and it's becoming harder to think of new things to write about for the magazine as well. If you'd like to keep up to date with all our goings-on then you can do so over on my blog. www.bustleandsew.com/blog.

I hope you have a lovely stitchy February.

Helen xx

Contents

The Month of February	Page 4	Lovebirds Softies	Page 29
Little Cupid Bear Embroidery	Page 5	Spring comes to the Garden	Page 32
Lovebirds Vintage Idea	Page 11	Snuggle Clothes Covers	Page 35
Lavender Handcream	Page 12	Vintage Crochet Throw	Page 40
Love Ewe Applique Cushion	Page 15	A Look at Applique	Page 43
Making Money from Making	Page 18	Applique Cardigans	Page 45
Making Money Making Bunnies	Page 21	Templates	Page 49
Homemade Lemonade	Page 27		

February, the second, and shortest, month of the year, takes its name from the Latin *februa,* a feast of expiation and purification held at this time in ancient Rome. Although the weather in February here in England can be some of the most unpleasant of the year - there's an old saying "as the days do lengthen, the cold do strengthen" which does seem to be true - the month does, however, give some tantalizing glimpses of the approach of spring with the gradual lengthening of the hours of daylight and first signs of new growth on plants and trees.

Today the best known feast day in February is the 14th - the day of St Valentine and lovers everywhere. But this isn't the only special day in the month. This year as Easter is so late Lent doesn't begin until March, but the 2nd of February sees the Feast of Candlemas commemorating the purification of Mary after the birth of Jesus. In times past, the Christmas season continued until Candlemas-eve when all the decorations would finally be taken down.

In the USA a weather-forecasting ritual takes place on 2nd February which is known as Groundhog day. This animal is said to emerge from hibernation on this day to check out the weather. If it's dull and wet he stays up and about because winter will soon be over, but if he can see his shadow then he'll go back to his burrow to sleep for another six weeks!

22nd February is George Washington's birthday. This US President was one of those people whose lifetime straddled the calendar reform of 1752 and whose date of birth therefore underwent a change. He was born on 11 February 1732, but didn't celebrate his 21st birthday until 22 February 1753, having "lost" eleven days in the changeover from the Julian calendar to the Gregorian calendar in September 1852!

February comes in like a sturdy country maiden, with a tinge of the red, hard winter apple on her healthy cheek, and as she strives against the wind, wraps her russet-coloured cloak well about her, while with bent head she keeps throwing back the long hair that blows about her face, and though at times half blinded by the sleet and snow, still continues her course courageously ....the mellow-voiced blackbird and the speckle-breasted thrush make music among the opening blossoms of the blackthorn, to gladden her way; and she sees faint flushings of early buds here and there, which tell her the long miles of hedgerows will soon be green.

Chambers Book of Days (1864)

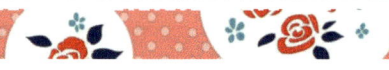

Little Cupid Bear Embroidery

This little bear is playing Cupid with his bow and arrow and buttoned-on wings! He doesn't seem too sure they'll be able to support his tubby body though, so is holding very tightly to the string of his balloon!

Shown mounted in 7" hoop.

Stitching notes:

- Two strands of floss are used throughout, except for the tiny stitch in white floss that makes the sparkle in the bear's eye - this is a single strand of floss.

- The balloon should be appliqued with short straight stitches placed at right-angles to the edge. Choose a floss that matches the fabric you're using.

- For the colours used for each part of the work see the photograph at the bottom of the page.

Stitches used:

Back stitch: text and balloon string

Satin stitch: hearts, arrow head, paw pads, harness around bear's body

Long & short stitch: wings

Chain stitch: bow

Fur: straight stitch - detailed notes for working fur follow.

Guidance for working these stitches can be found in my free e-book. Download from:

www.bustleandsew.com/free-patterns

You will need:

- 9" square background fabric - medium weight is best - quilting cotton is a bit light to take the dense fur stitching successfully

- 3" square cotton fabric for balloon

- DMC stranded cotton floss in colours: 304, 310, 400, 433, 436, 938, 966, 3812, 3849, 3864, 4240, blanc

- Bondaweb or temporary fabric spray adhesive

- 7" embroidery hoop - both for stitching and mounting as in photograph - I painted mine white before mounting my work.

Bear eye 310 sparkle in white
Nose 938

Bear harness 3812
Wings (light to dark) 966, 3849, 3812

Balloon string 4240
Bow, arrow head & hearts 304

Bear fur (light to dark) 436, 433, 400, 938

Paw pads 3864

Notes on stitching Bear:

Please excuse colour variations in photographs as I took them while I was stitching my bear - at different times of day and by different lights.

The first thing to consider when stitching fur is the direction of your stitches. If you have a pet, then take a look at them and you'll see that fur *always* grows away from the nose. Here's the bear with the direction of the fur stitches marked in red:

The second most important thing is the light and dark shading that gives a realistic 3-D effect to the fur. Decide where your light source will be - here I have imagined the sun is shining on the top of his head, so that will be the lightest fur, whilst the deepest shadows will be at the bottom of his tummy and legs. In general the right hand side will be darker than the left.

Features to the front are generally lighter than those behind, so the arm pulling the bow is lighter than the body behind, and the paw wrapped around the string is lighter than the rest of the arm.

This sounds a bit complicated but will become clearer in the stage by stage pictures.

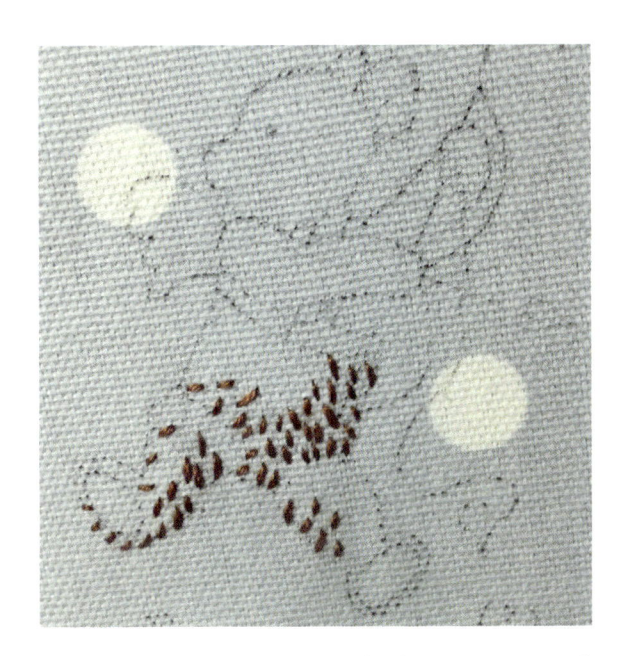

I always work my fur from the bottom upwards, so the stitches overlap in the same way that real fur would.

Begin by working a few stitches in 400 around the bottom of the tummy and legs, paying attention to their direction.

Continue up to his harness, you will work this bottom section of the bear first.

I've worked back stitch in 3812 along the edges of the harness (I will work satin stitch over these stitches later) and also a few stitches at the base of the wings - these will be shaded through 3 colours from dark nearest his body to light at the tips).

In this photo I've started to add the lightest brown, that's 436 and his fur's really starting to sparkle. You can overlap the stitches if you want, and make them slightly different lengths, this will all add to the fluffy feeling.

Beginning to fill in with 433 along the darkest areas of his body, and I've also satin stitched his paw pads in 3864.

Don't stitch along the outline of his body, work your stitches at an angle - this will look as though his fur is sticking out a little, nice and soft and fluffy! Continue with 433, and don't worry about making a mistake - the beauty of stitching fur this way is that you can always go back and layer more stitches over the top - this just makes the fur look more lush!

Here his body's nearly finished - don't worry if there are any small spaces you can always go back and fill them in later. Now add a few stitches in the very darkest brown (938) to help define the edges of his legs and create depth of shadow at the bottom of his body.

Work his harness in satin stitch over the top of the back stitch outline - this will help it stand out from the fur. Work his raised arm - keep the main part of the arm dark, then the paw curled around the string much lighter as it's in the foreground.

Add some of the darkest brown to his raised arm to help define the outline of the curled paw - and also the difference between the front and back arm. Start to work his head in the same way - stitch his eye in tiny straight stitches in black and his nose in dark brown - black is too harsh for his nose. Work your fur right up to them - you can always re-stitch them if they disappear into the fur while you're working.

Notice how the ear at the back is darker than the rest of his head and the stitches radiate from his eye and nose.

Working the arm at the front - again in exactly the same way as the rest of the body. See how the string meets the top of his paw then emerges across the top of the arm from the curled paw.

His top arm is finished. I've added the sparkle to his eye and two small French knots in 4240 to represent the buttons holding it closed. Look at the wings too - darkest nearest his body and pale at the tips as though the light was shining onto them.

When you work the bow - make two long stitches to represent the bowstring and take them into either side of his front paw as though he's pulling the bowstring.

10

Bustle & Sew

Love to Sew and Sew with Love …..

Vintage Lovebirds Applique

Sometimes it's fun to take a vintage transfer and give it a new lease of life with a different interpretation and here I've taken a vintage embroidery transfer and turned it into a cute cushion cover with some simple applique and stitching….

You'll find the original transfer in the templates section at the back of the magazine all ready for your own creativity to take over….

Lavender's blue, dilly dilly, lavender's green . . .

Last month we looked at using lavender, amongst other herbs to give our linens a beautiful, fresh fragrance. In this issue, as spring will soon be here and the gardening season begin again, I thought it would be fun to share my grandma's recipe for Gardeners' Lavender Hand Cream ....

If you're anything like me, you'll have the very best intentions of always wearing gloves when gardening - but somehow along the way they get put down and it's only when I realise how grubby my hands and nails have become and how cold they feel that I remember I was supposed to be wearing my gloves! You can purchase nice gardeners' hand cream, but this recipe is really easy to make as the ingredients are readily available from your local chemist or online. This makes quite a thick cream which becomes quite firm on cooling, so is best put into wide mouthed jars that are easy to reach into.

Gardeners' Lavender Hand Cream

The lavender oil used in this recipe adds a very slight perfume and it's also a powerful antiseptic and healing agent. The white wax is bleached bees' wax - available either in granules or as a block. If you can only get a block of wax, then grate it on the coarse side of a food grater or shred slivers off the block with a sharp knife. Coconut oil is extracted from the dried flesh of the coconut and has been used for centuries in lotions and creams to moisturise and condition skin and hair. Almond oil is one of the oldest known cosmetics and is a very light but effective oil which has no almond fragrance. It's still used in many commercially prepared cosmetics.

The amounts needed in this recipe are measured in spoons - just choose the size of spoon depending on the quantity you want to make:

- 4 spoons sweet almond oil
- 4 spoons coconut oil
- 3 spoons white wax
- 6 spoons glycerine
- Lavender essential oil (about 6 drops if you're using a tablespoon, otherwise adjust accordingly).

Put the almond oil, coconut oil and white wax in a double saucepan or a basin over a pan of hot water and gently dissolve them. Stir the mixture to blend everything together and when everything has melted, add the glycerine drop by drop. Remove from the heat and stir until creamy. Finally add drops of lavender oil and mix well. Put into pots and when cool screw lids on tightly.

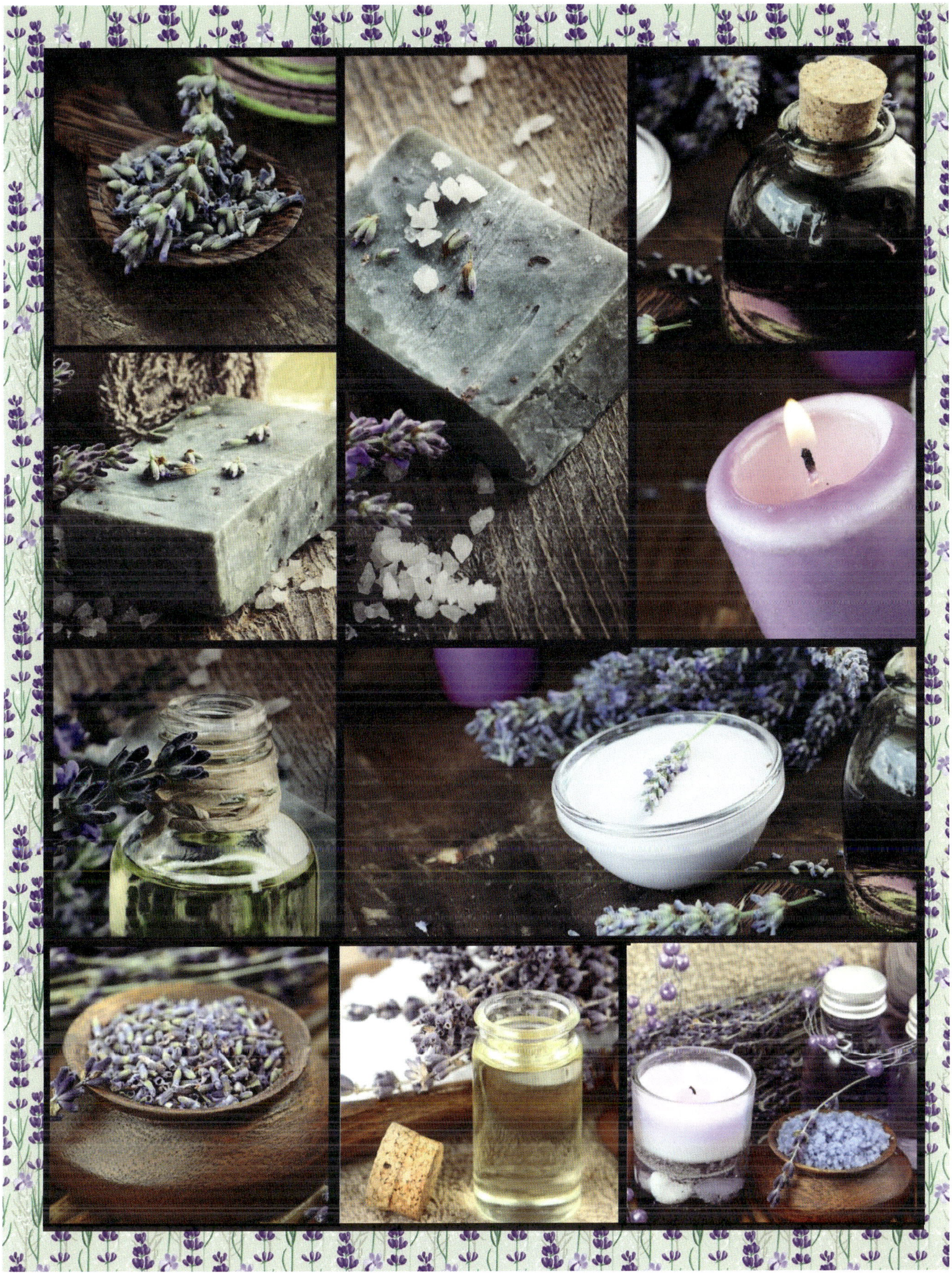

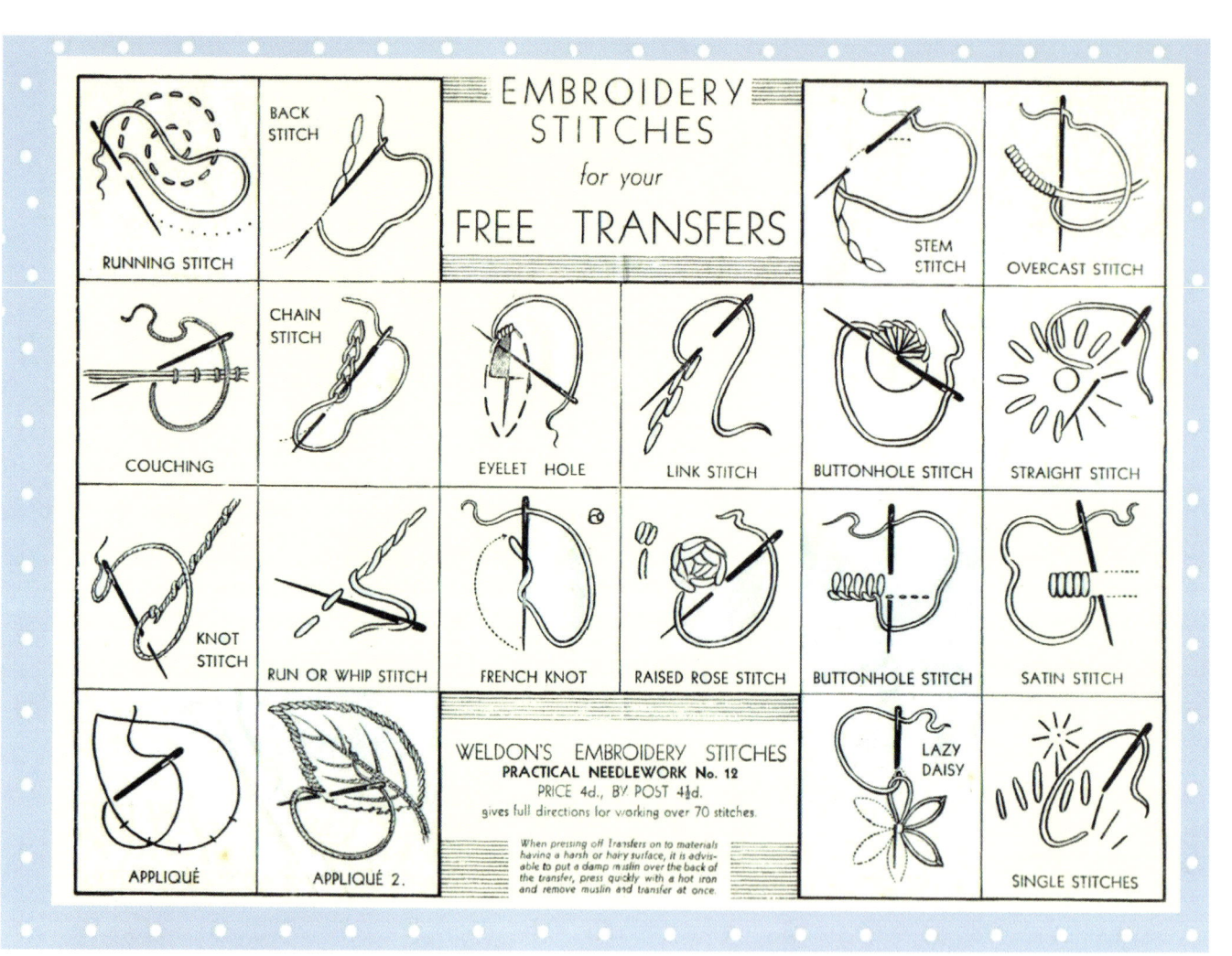

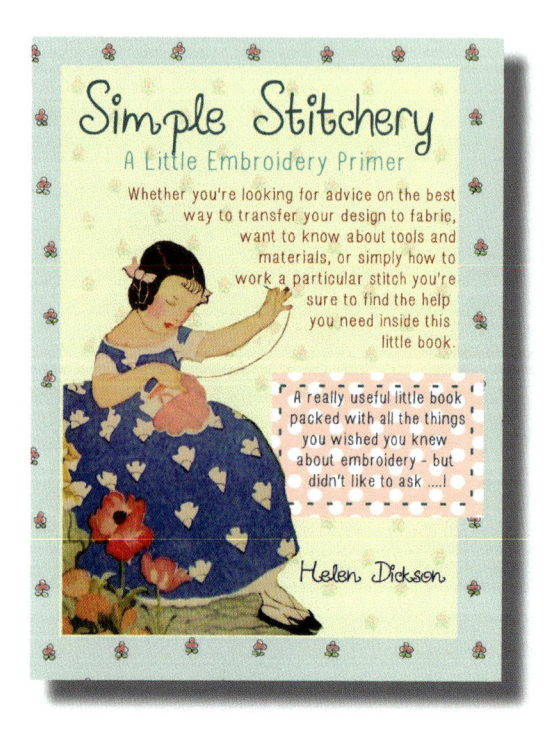

Here's a quick vintage reference to some of the most frequently used embroidery stitches. If you'd like a more detailed guide then please download my free e-book "Simple Stitchery" from the Free Patterns page of my website.

www.bustleandsew.com

It features a selection of stitches - and some cute illustrations from Flapdoodledesigns too.

Feather stitch!

Bustle & Sew

Love to Sew and Sew with Love .....

Love Ewe Applique Cushion

Here in south Devon we have lots of sheep - although none are quite as colourful as these! A simple effective design for Valentine's Day - or any time of year really, and a great way to use up your fabric scraps. Complete with easy freestyle machine applique, or you can always hand stitch if you prefer.

You will need:

- 18" square panel of medium weight non-stretchy fabric for front of cushion

- Two 18" x 12" rectangles of medium weight non-stretchy fabric for back of cushion

- Scraps of cheerful patterned fabric for the sheep (the templates are actual size so you'll be able to check whether your scraps are large enough)

- Scraps of black or dark grey felt for legs and faces

- Tiny scraps of red felt for hearts

- Small amount of pale pink stranded cotton embroidery floss (optional)

- Bondaweb

- Embroidery foot for your sewing machine

- Black or another dark colour and cream sewing thread

Applique Panel:

- Fold your 18" square into three lengthways and three sideways and lightly press the folds. Open up and smooth flat - you'll now have nine equal squares. This will help you position your sheep. The middle sheep is in the exact centre of the cushion and the others are towards the centre of their squares - this sounds a bit complicated - it's much easier to show you - please check out the following diagram. Doing this brings them more towards the front of the cushion so they don't get lost when the cushion's squashed!

- Trace 8 left facing and 1 right facing sheep onto the paper side of your Bondaweb. Cut roughly around the shapes.

- Fuse the shapes to the reverse of your patterned fabric and cut out the sheep bodies. Try to make nice smooth cuts - hold the scissors steady and move the fabric with your other hand.

- Repeat for the faces and legs. Extend the shapes as shown below so that the edges will be overlapped by the bodies:

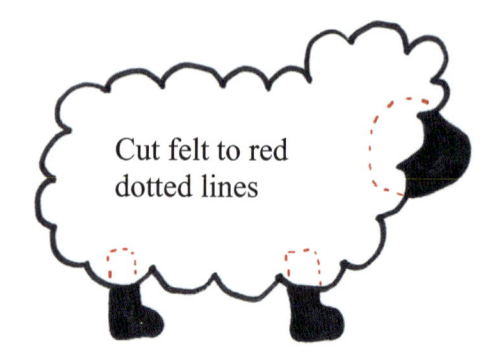

Cut felt to red dotted lines

- Peel the backing paper off the Bondaweb and arrange your sheep. When you're happy with their positioning place a lightweight cotton cloth over the top and press to fuse in place (the cloth will protect your felt from the hot iron).

- Cut two heart shapes from the red felt and fuse in place using the photographs as a guide.

- Now machine stitch all around the edges of the sheep. To do this fit the embroidery foot to your machine and drop the feed dogs. With cream thread in your bobbin and black or another dark colour in your needle go all around the shapes twice - not too neatly - you're aiming for a sort of scribbled effect.

- Just go around the edges of the hearts once as they're quite small and you don't want to swamp them in black thread.

- Press your work on the reverse and snip any thread ends. Stitch little pink cheeks on the blushing lovers - just a few small straight stitches. Your front panel is now complete.

Make up your cushion cover:

- Hem one long side on each of your 12" x 18" rectangles and press.

- Place your front panel right side up on a clean flat surface. Aligning the side edges, place your two rectangles on top with the hemmed edges towards the middle. There should be an approx 5" overlap at the centre - this forms the envelope closure where you'll insert your cushion pad.

- Pin or baste around the edges, then machine stitch. I usually go around twice for extra strength. Clip corners to remove excess bulk. Remove pins and turn right side out.

- Insert pad.

- FINSHED!!

Pin Cushion Mice

Discover more free patterns on the Bustle & Sew website www.bustleandsew.com

Making Money from Making

It's wonderful when you discover that it's actually possible to earn some money by doing something you love - like sewing! Over the next few issues I'm going to be offering you some hints and tips on successfully selling the items you love to make ...

As you probably know, I'm more than happy for you, as an individual stitcher and craftsperson, to use my patterns to make items for sale, as long as you credit Bustle & Sew with the design. After all, I don't make items for sale myself, and so it's lovely to think that others are using my patterns to bring pleasure to others. So, as the bazaar, fete and fair season approaches, and crafters begin to think about product lines for the summer, if you're considering starting selling your makes, or even if you already do so, I thought you might enjoy my tips for a creating or perhaps growing your own successful hobby-based enterprise.

What shall I make?

I guess my first tip would be sure to choose to make something you love - in fact I'm sure if you're reading this, then you're probably already sewing and making things that you're both good at and enjoy doing. But if you're serious about turning your hobby into even a very small business then you need to be really passionate about it, and have the enthusiasm to keep creating. If your business takes off, then you might find yourself needing to create 10, 20 or more of the same item, perhaps with just minor variations.

If you are the sort of person that constantly likes to move onto new things, then you may want to consider offering limited editions so you don't find yourself stitching your 45th pink felt chicken at midnight to fulfil demand!

And thinking about chickens …. it's absolutely vital that you research your market, and find out what your customers really want. You may love making purple velvet frogs, but find that they have a very limited market and that those pink felt chickens appeal to a much wider audience. Be sure to get some idea of what's popular before you begin creating - or you might be stuck with a large number of purple velvet frogs that cost you time and money to make, but that nobody wants to purchase.

You can market research both on and off-line - in fact the more methods you use to gather this information, the better!

Good ways to do this online are to visit websites already selling similar items to the ones you're thinking about making to sell. Browse around sites such as Etsy, Folksy, Notonthehighstreet, and Misi and you'll soon begin to discover popular items and identify trends. This isn't copying others, a definite big fat NO, it's simply getting a feel for what's on-trend at the moment. Visit social media sites such as Facebook and Twitter to find out what's out there and what people are commenting about them. You can even purchase from existing sites to see how their products compare to yours and get an idea of what they're doing well (Are their postage costs reasonable? Products nicely packaged? etc) and also not so well (Poor communication?). Then, if you decide to sell your makes online you'll have some ideas about what you like - and also dislike!

It's also a good idea to read homes and interiors magazines as again you'll quickly spot the latest trends and become aware of what everyone will be wanting for their homes this season. The good thing about being a small business is that you can respond to the market quickly, so if you spot that something's trending then you can offer items that satisfy current demand.

Try and go to craft and other handmade fairs, department stores and even just walk down the High Street studying shop window displays. Take a notebook around with you to jot down ideas - copying existing items is obviously totally wrong (and you could find yourself on the wrong side of copyright laws), but if you notice that, for example, woodland creatures are, then make a note and consider how you could offer foxes, owls and toadstools for sale - either your own design, or from a pattern whose designer is happy for you to sell items you make with their patterns. If you're not sure whether a designer allows you to do this - then all you need do is ask him or her.

And finally – ask your family and friends. They're going to be your most enthusiastic supporters and keen to ensure you make a success of your business. Ask them to be completely honest with you about your ideas and gather feedback on both the items you're making to sell and whether or not they think you'll be able to deliver – if yes to both of these– then that's great. If not – then ask them what the problems are and how they think you could overcome them.

What shall I call myself?

This isn't always an easy decision if you don't want to use your own name. I actually named Bustle & Sew after my two dogs at the time. Amy (my first Newfoundland) was a very girlie girl who loved to bustle around the house being busy and important, swishing her large black furry bum from side to side as she went. She also loved to lie on my feet as I sewed and so Amy gave me the "Bustle" part of my name.

At the time Ben was a young, slim dog (I'm sorry to say he's rather rounder now!!) who would slink around, curving his flexible body through amazingly small spaces. Obviously Bustle & Slink wasn't going to work. I stuck with the "S" of slink though, and changed it to Sew as sewing after all is what it's all about. In this way Bustle & Sew was born.

You can of course call your business anything you like – but I would recommend that you choose something that's easy to spell and that people will remember. Even if you don't plan on having your own website straight away its worthwhile checking that the domain name is available – and registering it if it's free – so that if, in time to come, you do decide to set up your own site, you don't find somebody else has taken your name. You can also protect your company name and logo with a trademark to ensure nobody else can use it – but that's perhaps something for the future?

Coming next month ….If you're planning to turn your hobby into a business you'll want to sell the items you make. The big question everybody asks at this point is "how much should I charge?"

Amy and Ben in 2008

Bustle & Sew

Love to Sew and Sew with Love .....

Making to Make: Bunnies

The craft fair season generally begins at Easter, though makers must begin preparations well before this. So this month I thought you might like some ideas using a simple bunny templates whether you're making for yourself or plan to sell your creations/

If you're making items to sell, whether for your own business or to raise funds for church, school or other cause, then it's important to offer items that are attractive, seasonal (if appropriate) and relatively quick and easy to make. These projects all use a simple bunny silhouette - perfect for those Easter events!

Two sizes of the silhouette are included in the templates section - there's the very small one that also includes the embroidery design for the floral garland, and also the smallest size for the set of three Easter bunnies. The larger templates would have taken too many pages to include. You can enlarge the silhouette to any size you require using a photocopier or, as it's a very simple outline, the old-fashioned grid method. (example on the next page).

The smallest bunny was created from the template in the templates section at the back of the magazine. I then increased the size of that template by 50% each time.

You will need:

- Three pieces of fabric for the bunny fronts to trace your template onto. You can make the back in the same fabric or, if you're trying to reduce costs, cut the backs from a plain fabric - vintage cotton sheets are nice for this as they're generally good quality and have a nice textural look.

- Toy stuffing

To make your bunnies:

- Print your templates at the size required and cut out a front and back for each bunny (remember to reverse your template if your fabric has a right and wrong side).

- Place the two pieces right sides together and pin or tack in place.

- Machine stitch all around the edge of the bunny leaving a 3" gap above the tail for stuffing. Take your time machine stitching, use a ¼" seam allowance and being very accurate so you will achieve a nice bunny shape.

- Clip curves and into corners. Turn right side out and roll seams between your fingers to make sure they're fully turned out before pressing your bunny shape.

- Stuff firmly and slipstitch gap closed. Finished!

Three Easter Bunnies

These are perhaps the easiest project of all. Their success depends entirely upon the accuracy of your machine sewing and good choice of fabrics.

Scaling your design using the grid method

Draw a small grid with equal squares over a tracing or copy of your design. Then draw an extended diagonal line through the corners of the grid to create an enlarged rectangle or square with the same proportions.   Draw another grid with the same number of squares as the first in the enlarged box, then copy the design as accurately as you can from the small to the large grid.

Bunny Cushions

Cushions are always very popular at fairs and here are two suggestions for bunny-themed creations. Again, as the designs are so simple, it's important that you concentrate on accuracy of stitching and fabric choices.

The large bunny cushion measures 18" to the top of his ears and the smaller patchwork cushion has a 16" pad.

You will need:

For large bunny:

- ¾ yard medium weight cotton or cotton/linen blend fabric
- 3" square pink felt for heart applique (optional)
- Bondaweb for heart applique (optional)
- Toy stuffing

For patchwork cushion:

- Nine x 5 ½" squares of cotton or cotton/linen blend fabric
- Two rectangles of cotton/cotton linen fabric each measuring 12" x 16" to make simple envelope back for cushion
- 14" square contrasting cotton fabric for bunny applique
- Temporary fabric marker pen
- Basting spray

To make large bunny cushion:

- Cut out two large shapes, remembering to reverse your template before cutting the second shape if your fabric has a right and wrong side.
- Cut two 3" strips across the width of your fabric and join together along one short edge. This is your gusset.
- Draw a heart shape onto the paper side of your bondaweb, cut out roughly and fuse to your pink felt. Apply to bunny using the photo as a guide - be sure to use a cloth to protect the felt from your hot iron. Machine zig-zag over edges using a matching or invisible thread. Press lightly.
- Starting 2" above the tail, attach gusset to front of bunny with a ¼" seam allowance. Take your time doing this as once again the accuracy of your stitching will determine how good your bunny will look. Clip curves and corners. Repeat for reverse of bunny, leaving a 3" gap for stuffing above the tail.
- Turn bunny right side out and press, rolling seams between fingers if necessary for them to turn out fully.
- Stuff firmly and slip stitch gap closed.

This shape would also make a good doorstop with the addition of a bag of rice or some pebbles at the base of the bunny.

To make patchwork cushion:

- With ¼" seam allowance join your squares into strips of three - then join the strips to make a square panel for the front of your cushion. Press seams on reverse.
- Draw around your template directly onto your bunny fabric using your temporary fabric marker pen. Carefully cut out shape and apply to centre of cushion with basting spray. Machine zigzag around edge in matching or invisible thread. (Don't use Bondaweb for this as it will be too expensive for such a large applique piece).

- Hem each of your fabric rectangles along one long side.

- Place your cushion front on a clean flat surface, right side uppermost. Place your rectangles face down on top aligning the side edges so they overlap in the centre. Pin then stitch around edges.

- Clip corners, turn right side out and press. Insert pad. Finished!

- Trace your bunny shape onto the paper side of your bondaweb, cut around roughly and fuse to the reverse of your floral fabric. Cut around shape, peel off backing paper and fuse to the centre of your square of fabric. Secure to fabric with short straight stitches worked in matching floss (I used 3839)

- Work your design in straight stitch, back stitch and French knots - see stitching guide.

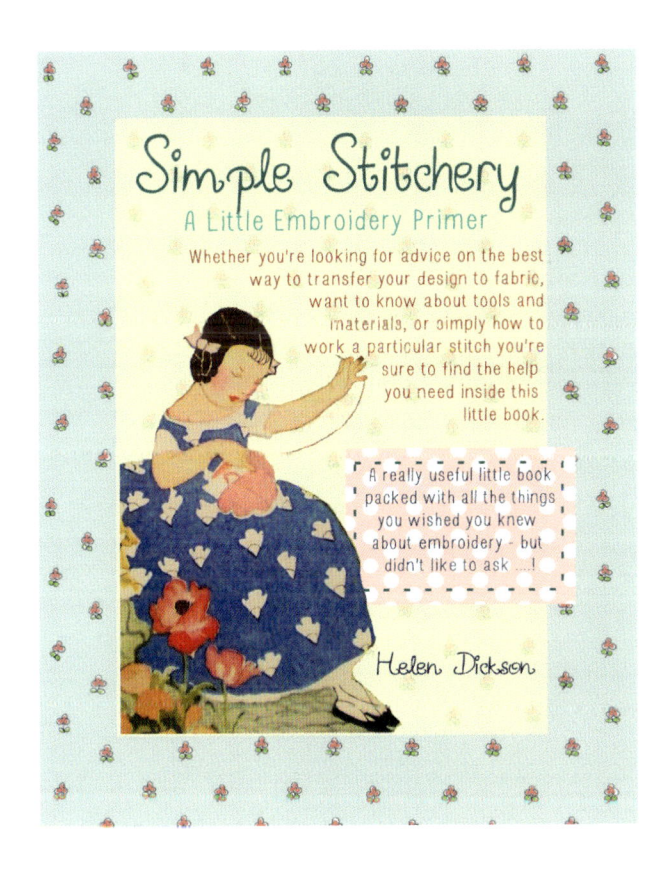

Floral Bunny Embroidery

Of all the bunny variations, this is the one that takes longest, though even this can be completed in 2 or 3 hours work. My bunny is shown mounted in a 7" hoop.

You will need:

- 10" square of white cotton fabric
- 5" x 4" piece of floral fabric for bunny
- DMC stranded cotton floss in colours 320, 368, 727, 796, 3354, 3839
- Bondaweb

Use two strands of floss throughout.

Method:

- Transfer the floral garland to your fabric, centering it in the middle of the square. I haven't given a reversed version as it really doesn't make any difference to this design.

For help and guidance on transferring your pattern and working the stitches you'll need, please download my free e-book "Simple Stitchery"

You'll find it on the free patterns page of the Bustle & Sew website.

www.bustleandsew.com/free-patterns

Colour	Number
Blue	368
Pink	320
Yellow-green	727
Green	3354
Light green	3839

The flowers are straight stitches radiating from the centre and the centres are small french knots colours as follows:

Yellow flowers 796
Pink flowers 3839
Blue flowers 796

The leaves are straight stitches too

26

There was once a great belief in the power of taking a spring tonic to wake up your body and get yourself moving again after the short dark days and long sleepy nights of winter. Lemons were very much part of this idea - whether as a hot lemon drink to comfort a cold-sufferer or homemade lemonade for children to enjoy. Lemonade is a simple pleasure and so easy to make at home. Although we think of it as a summer drink to be enjoyed on hot afternoons, it's packed full of vitamin C and is still a great pick-me-up when our immune systems are low at this time of year - a little bit of sunshine in a glass!

If you'd like to make lemonade to drink straight away then you can either use my grandma's recipe below, or make a French-style *citron presse* by just squeezing the juice of one lemon per person into a tall tumbler then adding sugar and water to taste. Stirring the mixture until the sugar dissolves is part of the pleasure of this simple drink.

Home made Lemonade

Take three juicy lemons and cut off the peel but no pith. Put the peel in a jug with three tablespoons of sugar and just cover with boiling water. Stir well then leave to cool. Squeeze the lemons and put the juice in the jug, then top up with cold water to taste.

Lemonade Syrup

This is a concentrated syrup that you can store for future lemonade making sessions. It can be bottled in sterilised bottles and sealed and will keep well in a cool place. Once you've opened the bottle then store in the fridge and use within a week.

You can use soda water or carbonated mineral water to top up the glass - or at this time of year hot water for a warming drink is very comforting too.

You will need:

- 5 small juicy lemons, scrubbed well
- 1 ½ lb (700g) cane sugar
- 1 pint (570 ml) boiling water
- 1 oz (25 g) tartaric acid

Method:

- Peel the lemons thinly with a sharp knife. Place the peel and sugar in a large bowl.
- Add the boiling water and stir well.
- Squeeze the lemons and add the juice and tartaric acid to the syrup.
- Leave to cool, then strain and bottle.
- Use about 2 tablespoons of syrup to each glass when mixing your lemonade.

Note:

When recipes call for using the whole of the lemon including the peel then it's best to use unwaxed lemons. If you can't get these, then scrub your lemons very well to remove the preservative wax.

Bustle & Sew

Love to Sew and Sew with Love .....

Lovebird Softies

These endearing little lovebirds are really easy to make and require only small amounts of fabric and felt (or use old blanket pieces or felted woollens as I have). And when they're so easy why limit yourself to two? Make a whole nestful for family and friends perhaps?

Finished birds measure 4" tall (approx)

For one bird you will need:

- 8" square felt for main body (or you can use felted woollens or old blanket - as long as they're not stretchy)
- 7" x 3" rectangle contrast felt for main body
- 6" square (or equivalent) of cotton floral fabric for wings and tail
- Tiny scraps of gold or yellow felt for beak
- Two ¾" buttons
- Two tiny (⅛") shiny spherical black buttons
- Rounded pebble/polybeads/rice to weight the tail end of base
- Toy stuffing
- Stranded cotton floss or cotton perle thread in a colour that works well with your fabric.
- Black thread to attach eyes

Cutting your pieces:

Cut out all pieces using the templates. These are actual size to make 4" high lovebirds, though there's no reason why you shouldn't make yours larger or smaller if you prefer. Cut pieces as follows:

- 2 x main body pieces in felt or felted woollen fabric
- 1 gusset piece in contrast felt
- 2 wings in main fabric
- 2 wings in floral fabric (reverse your template before cutting the second wing)
- 1 tail in main fabric
- 1 tail in floral fabric
- 2 x upper beak pieces
- 1 x lower beak piece

Notes on sewing:

I like to sew my softies by hand. I work with wrong sides together and make decorative (and strong) seams by stitching first one way in half-cross stitch then back again in the other direction to complete the stitch. Making them this way means I have complete control over shaping and stuffing the softie as I go along and, I think, gives a more "characterful" finish. Having said that, there are no tiny or narrow parts that would be difficult to turn, so if you wanted less obvious seams you could stitch them right sides together, then turn right way round and slip stitch your stuffing gap closed.

If you're using stranded cotton floss, sew your seams with 2 strands.

Make your Lovebird:

- Join the two main body pieces along the top from A to C and D to B, leaving C to D open as a gap for stuffing.

- Insert underbody gusset. Stuff your lovebird, starting at the beak end with tiny pieces of stuffing pushed well up into the pointy bit. Wrap your pebble in stuffing and position at the tail end of the bird so that he or she will sit up nicely when finished.

- Complete stuffing, making sure the bird is nice and firm, but not over stuffed. Use small pieces of stuffing and smooth and shape your bird with your hands as you go to ensure a nice shape and finish with no lumpiness.

- Sew the beak pieces together into a sort of pyramid shape matching the letters as shown on the templates. Push a tiny bit of stuffing into the tip of the beak, then place the beak on the head end of the bird matching z on the beak to z on the body pieces. (the beak will protrude beyond the end of the head piece). Secure in place with small straight stitches.

- Stitch the floral wing pieces together around edge as before, inserting a little stuffing before closing the seam - just enough to make the wing look nice and plump.

- Stitch buttons to floral sides of wings then position wings on sides of body and stitch in place using the photos as a guide to positioning. Take your thread right through the bird's body (a long needle is very helpful here) and pull fairly tightly so that the bottoms of the wings will spread outwards)

- Use glass-headed pins to determine the best position for your bird's eyes. Take your time over this as the positioning of the eyes makes such a difference to the character and expression of the finished bird. Then stitch the beads into place using black thread. Go right through the body and pull your thread fairly tight to mould the shape of the head and create little hollows for the eyes to sit in.

- Fold the tail in half and stitch onto the bottom end of the bird as shown in the photo.

Your bird is now finished!

Spring comes to the garden

From "The Secret Garden" by Frances Hodgson Burnett

"The Secret Garden" was first published in its entirety in 1911. It is one of Burnett's most popular novels, and is considered to be a classic of English children's literature.

On that first morning when the sky was blue again Mary wakened very early. The sun was pouring in slanting rays through the blinds and there was something so joyous in the sight of it that she jumped out of bed and ran to the window. She drew up the blinds and opened the window itself and a great waft of fresh, scented air blew in upon her. The moor was blue and the whole world looked as if something Magic had happened to it. There were tender little fluting sounds here and there and everywhere, as if scores of birds were beginning to tune up for a concert. Mary put her hand out of the window and held it in the sun.

"It's warm-warm!" she said. "It will make the green points push up and up and up, and it will make the bulbs and roots work and struggle with all their might under the earth."

She kneeled down and leaned out of the window as far as she could, breathing big breaths and sniffing the air until she laughed because she remembered what Dickon's mother had said about the end of his nose quivering like a rabbit's.

"It must be very early," she said. "The little clouds are all pink and I've never seen the sky look like this. No one is up. I don't even hear the stable boys."

A sudden thought made her scramble to her feet. "I can't wait! I am going to see the garden!"

She had learned to dress herself by this time and she put on her clothes in five minutes. She knew a small side door which she could unbolt herself and she flew down-stairs in her stocking feet and put on her shoes in the hall. She unchained and unbolted and unlocked and when the door was open she sprang across the step with one bound, and there she was standing on the grass, which seemed to have turned green, and with the sun pouring down on her and warm sweet wafts about her and the fluting and twittering and singing coming from every bush and tree. She clasped her hands for pure joy and looked up in the sky and it was so blue and pink and pearly and white and flooded with springtime light that she felt as if she must flute and sing aloud herself and knew that thrushes and robins and skylarks could not possibly help it. She ran around the shrubs and paths toward the secret garden.

"It is all different already," she said. "The grass is greener and things are sticking up everywhere and things are uncurling and green buds of leaves are showing."

The long warm rain had done strange things to the herbaceous beds which bordered the walk by the lower wall. There were things sprouting and pushing out from the roots of clumps of plants and there were actually here and there glimpses of royal purple and yellow unfurling among the stems of crocuses. The long warm rain had done strange things to the herbaceous beds which bordered the walk by the lower wall. There were things sprouting and pushing out from the roots of clumps of plants and there were actually here and there glimpses of royal purple and yellow unfurling among the stems of crocuses. Six months before Mistress Mary would not have seen how the world was waking up, but now she missed nothing.

When she had reached the place where the door hid itself under the ivy, she was startled by a curious loud sound. It was the caw-caw of a crow and it came from the top of the wall, and when she looked up, there sat a big glossy-plumaged blue-black bird, looking down at her very wisely indeed. She had never seen a crow so close before and he made her a little nervous, but the next moment he spread his wings and flapped away across the garden. She hoped he was not going to stay inside and she pushed the door open wondering if he would. When she got fairly into the garden she saw that he probably did intend to stay because he had alighted on a dwarf apple-tree, and under the apple-tree was lying a little reddish animal with a bushy tail, and both of them were watching Dickon, who was kneeling on the grass working hard.

Mary flew across the grass to him. "Oh, Dickon! Dickon!" she cried out. "How could you get here so early! How could you! The sun has only just got up!"

He got up himself, laughing and glowing, and tousled; his eyes like a bit of the sky. "Eh!" he said. "I was up long before him. How could I have stayed abed! Th' world's all fair begun again this mornin', it has. An' it's workin' an' hummin' an' scratchin' an' pipin' an' nest-buildin' an' breathin' out scents, till you've got to be out on it 'stead o' lyin' on your back. When th' sun did jump up, th' moor went mad for joy, an' I was in the midst of th' heather, an' I run like mad myself, shoutin' an' singin'. An' I come straight here. I couldn't have stayed away. Why, th' garden was lyin' here waitin'!"

Seeing him talking to a stranger, the little bushy-tailed animal rose from its place under the tree and came to him, and the rook, cawing once, flew down from its branch and settled quietly on his shoulder. They ran from one part of the garden to another and found so many wonders that they were obliged to remind themselves that they must whisper or speak low.

He showed her swelling leaf-buds on rose branches which had seemed dead. He showed her ten thousand new green points pushing through the mould. They put their eager young noses close to the earth and sniffed its warmed springtime breathing; they dug and pulled and laughed low with rapture until Mistress Mary's hair was as tumbled as Dickon's and her cheeks were almost as poppy red as his.

There was every joy on earth in the secret garden that morning, and in the midst of them came a delight more delightful than all, because it was more wonderful. Swiftly something flew across the wall and darted through the trees to a close grown corner, a little flare of red-breasted bird with something hanging from its beak. Dickon stood quite still and put his hand on Mary almost as if they had suddenly found themselves laughing in a church.

"We munnot stir," he whispered in broad Yorkshire. "We munnot scarce breathe. I knowed he was mate-huntin' when I seed him last. It's Ben Weatherstaff's robin. He's buildin' his nest. He'll stay here if us don't flight him."

They settled down softly upon the grass and sat there without moving.

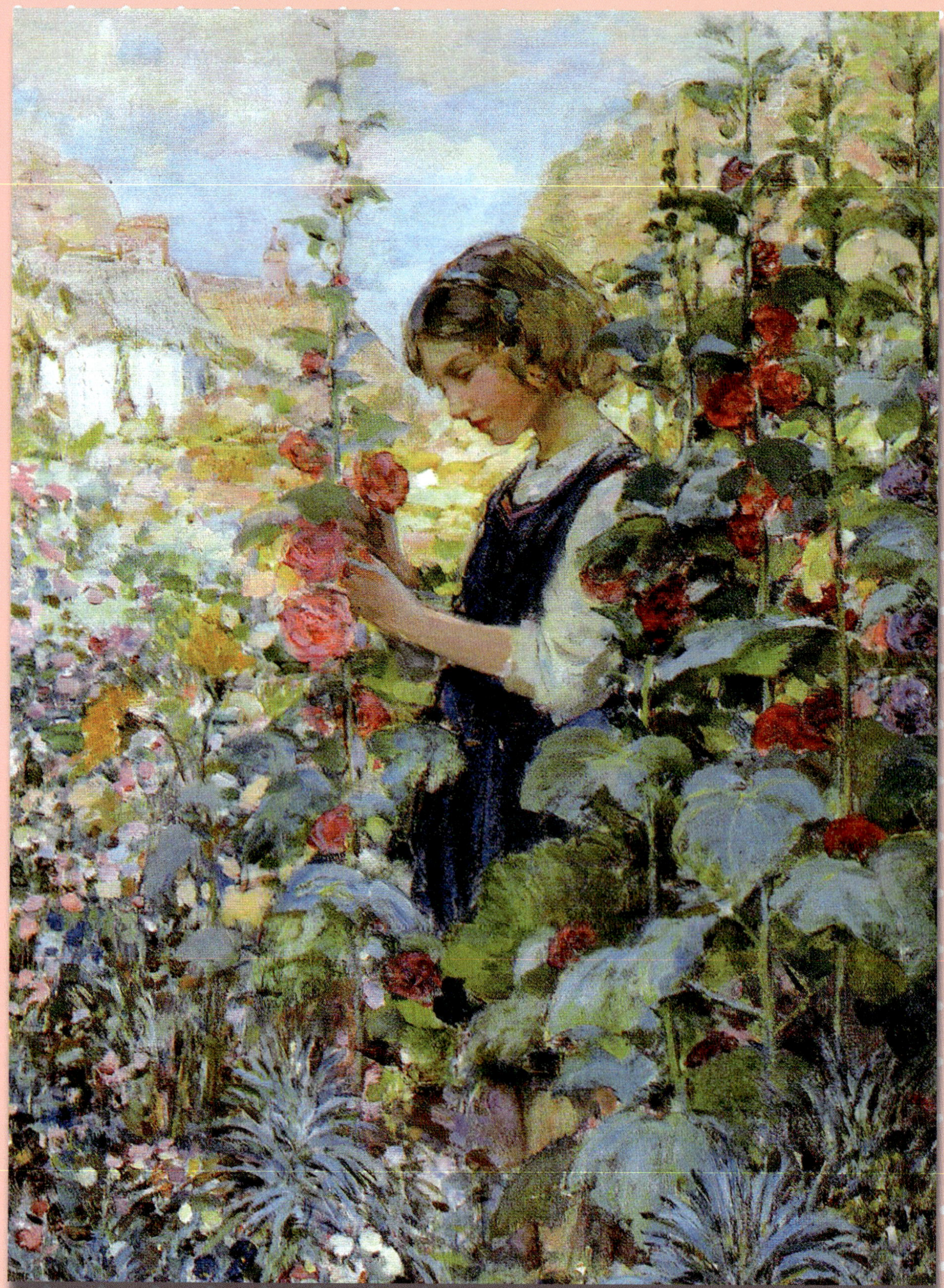

Bustle & Sew

Love to Sew and Sew with Love .....

Snuggle Clothes Covers

Your winter woollies and party frocks will be able to snuggle down for a long summer's sleep beneath these hanger covers. Hanging on padded hangers is pretty - and also helps prevent stretching and distortion of delicate fabrics.

Please note: this pattern is for the covers and padded hanger, not the applique cardigans.

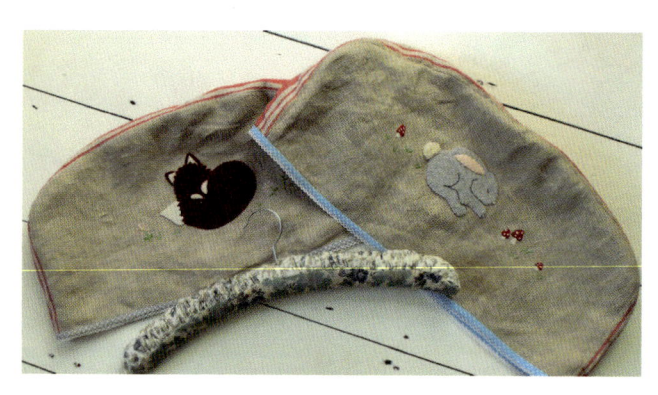

You will need:

For the padded hanger:

- 24" x 7" rectangle light or quilting weight cotton fabric (hanger top)
- 12" x 7" rectangle light or quilting weight cotton fabric (hanger bottom)
- Two 8 ½" x 4 ½" (approx) pieces of lightweight cotton or polyester quilt batting
- Strong thread
- Plain wooden hanger - you could possibly use strong plastic, but wood is definitely best.
- Small amount of toy stuffing

For one cover:

- 20" square of light to medium weight plain linen or linen/cotton mix fabric for outer
- 35" x 2 ½" strip of the same fabric for the gusset
- 20" square of light to medium weight patterned linen or linen/cotton mix fabric for lining
- 35" x 2 ½" strip of the same fabric for the gusset
- 44" bias binding (one with a lace trim like mine does look lovely, but plain will work just fine)
- Temporary fabric marker pen
- Bondaweb

For the sleepy bunny cover:

- 4 ½" x 3 ½" grey felt
- Tiny piece of pale pink felt
- Tiny scrap of fake fleece for tail
- Stranded cotton floss in pale pink and grey (to match your felt), also cream, red, dark grey and green

For the sleepy fox:

- 5" x 4 ½" reddish brown felt
- Scraps of cream felt
- Stranded cotton floss in reddish brown and cream (to match your felt), also black, pale pink, light yellow and green

To make the padded hanger:

- Fold your top fabric in half lengthways so you have a 24" x 3 ½" rectangle. Round off one end - use a suitably sized lid and draw around it with your fabric marker pen. Cut along the line, then along the fold so you finish with two long rectangles, each with a rounded shape at one end.

- Repeat this process with the bottom fabric.

- Turn under ½" on the short straight edge of each hanger top and bottom and press firmly into place (there's no need to stitch them)

- Make two rows of gathering stitches (a long machine stitch is fine) ¼" in from the edge along the long sides of each hanger top section from the turned under end to within 1 ¼" of the rounded end.

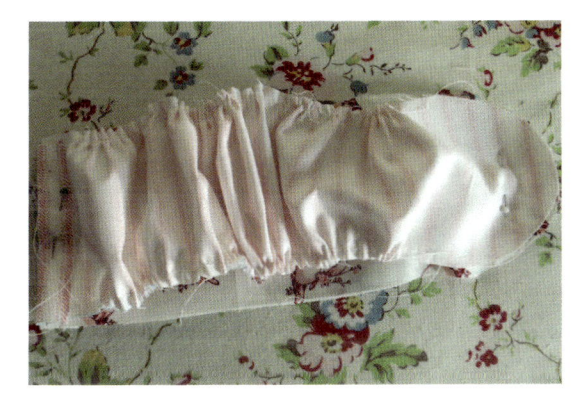

- With right sides together, pin one hanger top to one hanger bottom, pulling up the gathers to fit. Baste or pin firmly together then stitch all around the edge with a ½" seam allowance leaving the straight short edge open. Trim seams, clip the curved end and turn right side out. Repeat with the other hanger top.

- Wrap the batting around the wooden arms of the hanger - check to make sure it will fit snugly - but not too tightly - within the two sleeves you've created. Secure in place with strong thread wrapped around and tied tightly.

- Push a little toy stuffing into the end of each hanger sleeve.

- Slip the sleeves over each arm of the hanger with the gathered side on top.

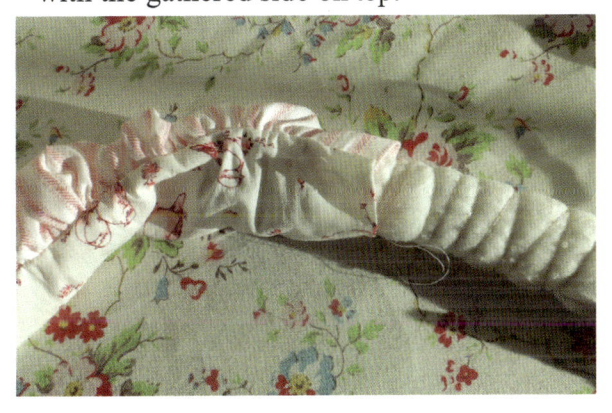

- Slipstitch the turned under edge of the sections together.

- Your padded hanger is now finished.

To make the clothes cover:

- First you'll need to make a template for the front and back of the cover. Fold your fabric in half and place your hanger just down from the fold. With your temporary marker pen draw along the top of the hanger, following its shape.

- Extend your line 2" out from each end of the hanger, then draw a vertical line down for another 8" at each end. Join along the bottom to create the shape of your cover front. Cut out through both thicknesses of fabric. Use this shape as the pattern to cut out the lining.

- Place the lining pieces and one of the outer panels to one side for the moment and work the applique decoration on the front piece. The applique is very simple to create:

- Bunny

Trace the body shape onto the paper side of your Bondaweb. Cut out roughly then fuse to the grey felt and cut out the bunny shape. Position on the front panel centrally and 3 ¼" down from the top edge. Fuse into place. Repeat with the ear - you may wish to use a cloth to protect the felt from your hot iron. Secure applique shape to main panel with short straight stitches worked in two strands of your matching floss at right angles to the edge of the shape.

Draw the shape of the legs and eye onto the bunny using your temporary fabric marker pen and work in back stitch using two strands of dark grey floss. Stitch the nose in pale pink satin stitch and the whiskers are long stitches worked in a single strand of cream floss. Cut out the tail shape and stitch into place.

Draw simple toadstools and grass around the bunny and stitch using 2 strands of floss. The toadstools are worked in long and short stitch and the spots are satin stitch worked at right angles to the long and short stitch. The grass is stem stitch.

When your applique is finished, remove any marker pen lines and press lightly on the reverse being careful not to flatten his tail.

- Fox

Trace the body shape onto the paper side of your Bondaweb, omitting the ears. Trace the ears (both inner and outer separately allowing a little extra to underlap the body shape, also trace the face markings and the tail tip. Fuse the main body and outer ears onto your reddish brown felt and the inner ears, face markings and tail tip onto cream felt.

Position on the front panel centrally and 3 ¼" down from the top edge. Make sure the head overlaps the edges of the ears. Position all your pieces before fusing and only press with a hot iron when you're happy with how they look. (Don't forget to protect your felt with a cloth). Secure applique shapes with 2 strands of matching floss and short straight stitches worked at right angles to the edges of the shape.

Draw the shape of the tail and eyes onto the fox using your temporary fabric marker pen and work in back stitch using two strands of black floss. Stitch the nose in black satin stitch.

Draw simple flowers and grass around the fox and stitch using two strands of floss. The flowers have a cluster of small French knots in pale yellow at the centres (you could use satin stitch if preferred) and pink lazy daisy petals. The grass is stem stitch.

When you've finished remove all temporary lines and press lightly on the reverse.

Make up the cover:

- Round off the top corners of your cover (both lining and exterior panels) by drawing around and approx 3" diameter lid and cutting along the lines.

- With right sides together and a ¼" seam allowance stitch the gusset along the outer edges of the front panel of the cover around the top from A to B. Repeat for back of cover, clip curved edge then press seams. Turn the right way round

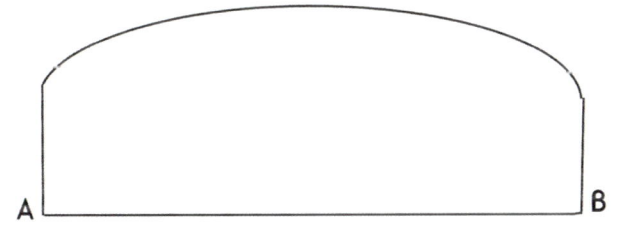

Leave bottom edge open

- Repeat with cover lining, but leave with wrong sides on the outside. Slide the lining up inside the exterior and pin or baste in place.

- Bind along bottom edge with bias binding.

- Fold your lining in half widthways and press lightly with your hands. Open up and where the fold comes make the opening for the hanger hook in the centre of the gusset - this is a ½" buttonhole made through both the lining and the gusset.

- Your cover is now finished.

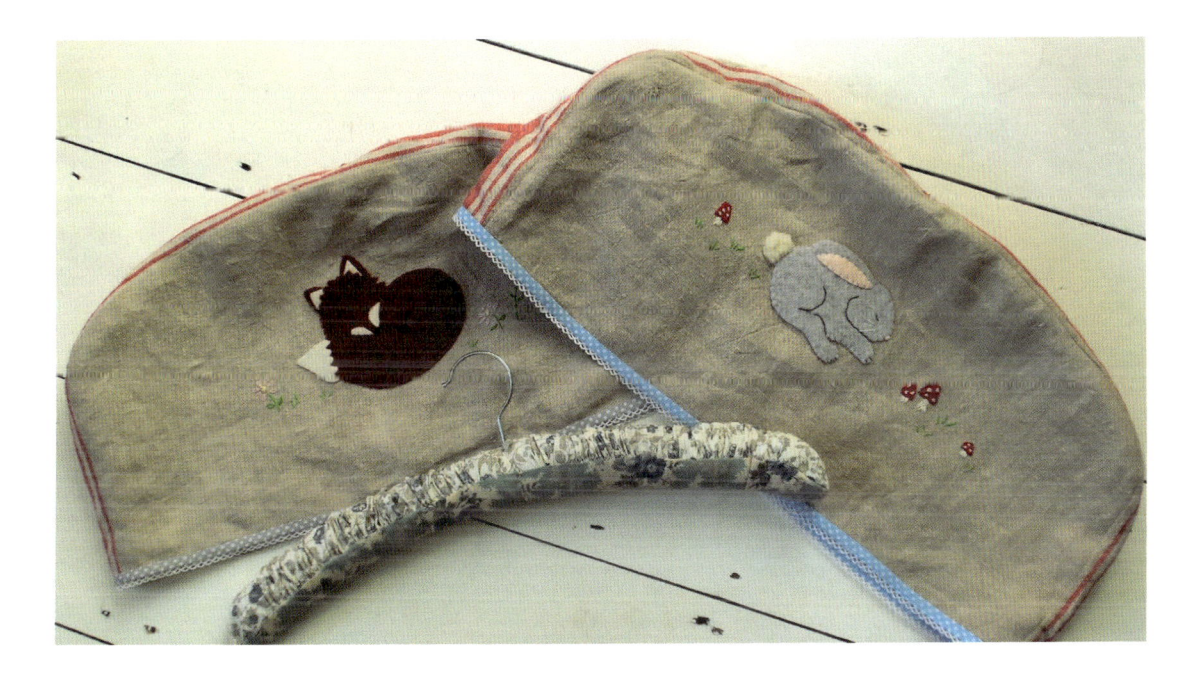

Vintage Crochet Throw

Crochet has seen an amazing revival in popularity and this vintage pattern is as fresh and colourful today as it was when first published….

MEASUREMENTS
83 x 101cm/32¾ x 39¾in

MATERIALS
8 x 50g balls of wool-mix DK in cream; approximately 400g of wool, wool mix, cotton and cotton-mix DK yarn in as many shades as possible of pink, fuchsia, red, maroon, purple, blue, green, lime, olive, turquoise, gold and orange. Size 2.50 and 3.50 crochet hooks.

TENSION
Each complete motif measures 9 x 9cm, using 3.50 hook.

ABBREVIATIONS
Ch, chain; **dc**, double crochet; **st**, stitch; **tr**, treble; **dtr**, double tr; **htr**, half treble; **sp**, space; **slst**, slip st, **yrh**, yarn round needle.

NOTE
Instructions in square brackets are worked as stated after second bracket.

ROSE MOTIF

Make 49 motifs, each time using a different combination of the following shades: pink, fuchsia, red, lilac, purple, lime, pale green, olive, blue green and mid green. With 3.50 hook, make 5ch, slst in first ch to form ring.

1st round: 1ch, 8dc in ring, slst in first dc.
2nd round: 1ch, 2dc in same place as slst, 2dc in each of next 7dc, change to second colour and slst in first dc — 16dc.
3rd round: 1dc in same place as slst, [3ch, 3tr in next dc, withdraw hook and reinsert it in top of first tr, catch dropped loop and pull through firmly, 3ch, 1dc in next dc] 7 times, 3ch, 3tr in next dc, withdraw hook and reinsert it in top of first tr, catch dropped loop and pull through firmly, 3ch, change to third colour and slst in first dc.
4th round: 4ch, 3dtr in same place as slst, [1ch, 4dtr in next dc] 7 times, 1ch, slst in 4th ch. Fasten off.
With right side facing, join in cream to a 1chsp.
5th round: 4ch, 1tr in same sp as join, [4ch, 2dc in next 1chsp, 4ch, work 1tr, 1ch and 1tr in next 1chsp] 3 times, 4ch, 2dc in next 1chsp, 4ch, slst in 3rd ch.
6th round: 2ch, work 1tr, 1ch and 1tr in first 1chsp, 1htr in next tr, [4dc in next 4chsp, 1dc in each of next 2dc, 4dc in next 4chsp, 1htr in next tr, work 1tr, 1ch and 1tr in next 1chsp, 1htr in next tr] 3 times, 4dc in next 4chsp, 1dc in each of next 2dc, 4dc in next 4chsp, slst in 2nd ch. Fasten off.

DAISY MOTIF

Make 50 motifs using a different combination each time of following shades: blue, lilac, purple, orange, gold, lime, olive, bright green, pale green and turquoise.

With 3.50 hook, make 6ch, slst in first ch to form ring.

1st round: 1ch, 12dc in ring, change to second colour and slst in first dc.

2nd round: 4ch, 1dtr in same place as slst, 2dtr in each of next 11dc, slst in 4th ch — 24 sts. Fasten off.

With right side facing, join in third colour between two pairs of dtr.

3rd round: 2ch, yrh, insert hook in same place as join, yrh and pull through, yrh and pull through 2 loops on hook, yrh, insert hook in same place again, yrh and pull through, yrh and pull through 2 loops on hook, yrh, and pull through 3 loops on hook, * 3ch, yrh, insert hook in between next two pairs of dtr, yrh and pull through, yrh and pull through 2 loops on hook, [yrh, insert hook in same place again, yrh and pull through, yrh and pull through 2 loops on hook] twice, yrh, and pull through 4 loops on hook, repeat from * 10 times more, 3ch, slst in top of second stitch. Fasten off.

With right side facing, join in cream to a 3chsp.

4th round: 1ch, 4dc in 3chsp, [work 2tr, 1ch, 2tr in next 3chsp, 4dc in each of next two 3chsps] 3 times, work 2tr, 1ch and 2tr in next 3chsp, 4dc in last 3chsp, slst in first dc.

5th round: 1ch, 1dc in each of first 4dc, [1dc in next tr, 1htr in next tr, work 1tr, 1ch and 1tr in 1chsp, 1htr in next tr, 1dc in next tr, 1dc in each of next 8dc] 3 times, 1dc in next tr, 1htr in next tr, work 1tr, 1ch and 1tr in 1chsp, 1htr in next tr, 1dc in next tr, 1dc in each of last 4dc, slst in 1st dc.

TO MAKE UP

Press motifs lightly on wrong side. Starting with daisy motif and alternating motifs, arrange them to form a rectangle nine motifs wide and 11 motifs long. With right sides of motifs together, using 3.50 hook and cream, join motifs as arranged with row of dc, working 1ch between each joined and following pair.

Edging: With right side facing and using 3.50 hook, join cream in corner 1chsp.

1st round: 1ch, 3dc in same sp as join, * 1dc in each of next 14 sts, ** [yrh, insert hook in next 1chsp, yrh and draw through, yrh and draw through 2 loops on hook] twice, yrh and draw through 3 loops on hook, 1dc in each of next 14 sts **, repeat from ** to ** to next corner, 3dc in corner 1chsp ***, repeat from * to *** twice more, 1dc in each of next 14 sts, repeat from ** to ** to last corner, slst in first dc. Change to 2.50 hook and work 1 round of crab st (dc worked from left to right), slst in first dc. Fasten off.

The **FARMER'S** *Magazine* **WIFE**

MAY
1937

Spring is on the way!!

APPLIQUE

Applique is named after the French term "appliquer" - it's a verb that means "to apply". In its broadest sense it means an ornament or decoration that's applied to any surface - though of course in sewing it means cutting a fabric shape and attaching it to your background fabric to create a decorative effect. The shapes are applied using either spray adhesive or fusible webbing, such as Bondaweb and then secured and possibly decorated with hand or machine stitching. Applique is one of my favourite techniques that I use in lots of my patterns so I thought it might be useful to quickly run through the process.

For smaller pieces I like to use fusible webbing. This is an iron-on fabric adhesive that you purchase either on a roll or in pre-cut pieces. The adhesive side is backed with paper that can be drawn on so you can easily trace the shape you want to apply. The actual adhesive is a very thin layer of glue that melts when you fuse it to your background fabric with a hot iron. It's really easy to use if you follow these stages:

- Trace your shape onto the paper side of the fusible webbing. I always provide pieces to be appliqued in reverse - so when you've traced and fused they will come out the right way round! Be sure to trace the shape accurately as this will be your only guide for cutting out your applique piece. Cut out your shape roughly.

- With the paper side uppermost, iron the fusible webbing (Bondaweb) onto the reverse side of the applique fabric. The glue on the Bondaweb will melt in the heat of the iron, so be careful not to accidentally touch the glue side with your iron plate or you'll end up with a nasty sticky mess. (an an iron that needs cleaning too!)

- Once you've fused the Bondaweb to the reverse of your applique fabric you can cut out your shape accurately along the lines you drew. Always hold your scissors steady in one hand and move the fabric around making long smooth cuts with the scissors. It's much easier than trying to move the scissors - this may take a little practise, but in the long run you will achieve much better results.

- When you've cut out your shape then carefully peel off the backing paper and apply the motif onto your background fabric. If you have trouble peeling off the paper try scratching the back with the tip of a pin to score the paper, then you should be able to easily peel it away.

If you're building up a multi-layered design then don't fuse the pieces until you're completely happy with their placing - once fused they're extremely hard to remove (and almost impossible without damaging them). Pieces at the back of the design should be overlapped by those further forward.

Always secure the edge of the applique shape by stitching - either by hand or by machine. Machine applique is a great fun technique and gives really professional-looking results very easily once you've mastered the basics.

Hints for great machine applique:

- Make sure your needle is nice and sharp as you'll be asking it to go through a lot of layers.

- Use a medium weight background fabric without a hoop, or if you're using a lighter weight hoop up in reverse before stitching so that it doesn't pucker.

- Drop your feed dogs (if you're unsure how to do this then refer to your machine's user manual) and fit an embroidery foot. This isn't essential but is good for safety reasons if nothing else.

- You may need to reduce your top tension a little, it's worth practising on some scrap fabric first.

- Use a pale coloured thread in the bobbin and darker in the needle. This gives a less solid stitched line.

- Be sure to drop your presser foot - although the embroidery foot doesn't hold the fabric firm it's important to drop it to get the needle tension correct.

- To begin, pull your thread up to the top, sew a couple of stitches on top of each other and then cut the threads to prevent tangling or overstitching the tail end (again almost impossible to get out if the needle splits the thread).

- If you've overlapped shapes then you'll only need to stitch one edge. For example, in the cupcake at the top of this page, the cake piece is overlapped by the cake case, so I only stitched the edge of the case.

- Machine stitching is also great for decorating your shapes - see the cake case above and cup to the left. Draw the lines on first with temporary marker pen and then stitch over them.

Applique Cardigans

Sometimes a cardie can be just a little plain! I love to give my woollies a designer touch - it's so easy to do and everyone will want to know where yours came from…

Always start with a good quality knitted, it's really not worth spending time and effort on a cheap item. I love Woolovers woollies - they ship worldwide (at the moment there's free worldwide delivery too!) and are very reasonably priced.

www.woolovers.com

Following all the lovely comments I received about my Autumn Hedgerows Applique Cardigan in the October 2013 issue, I thought I'd include another couple of ideas for spring cardigans to show how easy it is to turn a relatively ordinary mass produced item into something that's really rather special - and that you know nobody else will be wearing wherever you go!

I've always loved applique childrenswear - and remember my mum, so many years ago, patching the knees of my dungarees not with squares of fabric, but with rabbits, trees and yes - flowers too. But why should kids have all the fun? I thought - why not applique for grown-ups too? To avoid looking like a rather large child, it's a good idea to keep your applique to just an accent point, and choose a limited selection of colours or, as I have in the pink cardigan, small areas cut from a larger design that work really well with the colour of your cardigan.

I used a selection of felted woollens and some wool-blend felt for my toadstools. Whatever you decide upon make sure that you pre-wash all your fabrics - and your cardigan too - and that in future they can all be washed at the same temperature. Ideally you should choose fabrics that won't fray and they MUST - I can't emphasise this strongly enough so I'll type it again - they MUST be nonstretchy - it's impossible to machine applique stretchy fabrics. If your fabric is the sort that frays, then you can apply fraycheck if you think it might be a problem - it shouldn't in any case fray inside the line of machine stitching.

The grass is worked in two shades of green crewel wool and the spots in 2 strands of cream cotton embroidery floss.

For the toadstools you will need:

- Good quality wool or wool-blend cardigan
- Selection of wool or wool-blend fabrics
- Bondaweb
- Sewing thread - use a colour that matches your cardigan in the bobbin and black in the needle
- Darning foot for your sewing machine.
- Six replacement buttons for your cardigan if you don't like the existing ones - I chose a pale wood colour.

Be sure to keep the buttons - I've saved the grey shell ones from my cardigan - they are a lovely quality but I just didn't like them very much. But they're sure to come in handy for a future project!

For the florals you will need:

- Good quality wool or wool-blend cardigan
- Bondaweb
- Darning foot for your sewing machine
- Sewing thread - use a colour that matches your cardigan in the bobbin and invisible thread in the needle.
- Six replacement buttons for your cardigan - I found some lovely pale pink ones with white dots.

Method:

- Pre-wash all fabrics and your cardigan.
- Trace the templates onto the paper side of your Bondaweb, cut around roughly then fuse to the reverse of your applique fabrics. Cut out shapes and position on cardigan. Don't fuse into place immediately - cut them all and play around with the positioning until you're happy with the design.
- When you're happy with the positioning of your shapes you'll need to fuse them to your cardigan. Be sure to protect your woollen with a cotton cloth and don't move the iron - a press down with moderate pressure and a burst of steam works well. Then turn your knitwear inside out and press the same area from the reverse, again protecting the wool from the iron with a cloth. This will make sure your shapes are really well fuse and so the area you'll be machine stitching won't be stretchy - the shapes will act as a stabiliser for the knitted fabric beneath.

- Make sure your cardigan is dry and cool before beginning to machine stitch. If it's damp and warm it is more likely to stretch out of shape.
- Then fit the darning foot to your machine and drop your feed dogs. Stitch twice around the edges of your shapes with a sketchy looking line - don't be too neat. Be sure to support the whole weight of your cardigan on your sewing machine table when you're stitching - you don't want to run any risk of the knitted fabric stretching or distorting.
- Because the feed dogs are dropped you shouldn't need a fabric stabiliser as they're not exerting any "pull" on the knitted fabric. You can use a light-weight fusible interfacing as stabiliser, but if you can get by without, as I did, then I'd recommend doing so as this gives a much nicer finish on the reverse.
- When you've finished stitching, press lightly with a cool iron. Darn in all the loose ends securely. Wear cardigan and wait for compliments!!

Twelve copies of the Bustle & Sew Magazine

Back copies available from the Bustle & Sew website.

www.bustleandsew.com

Pattern Templates

Cupid Bear Embroidery

Transfers are actual size and both ways round to suit your preferred method of transfer.

Friendship is Love without his wings.

Friendship is Love without his wings.

Vintage Lovebirds

Original mid-century design.

Love Ewe Applique Cushion Cover

Templates are actual size

Cut 8 sheep facing left

Cut 1 sheep facing right

Lovebirds templates (actual size)

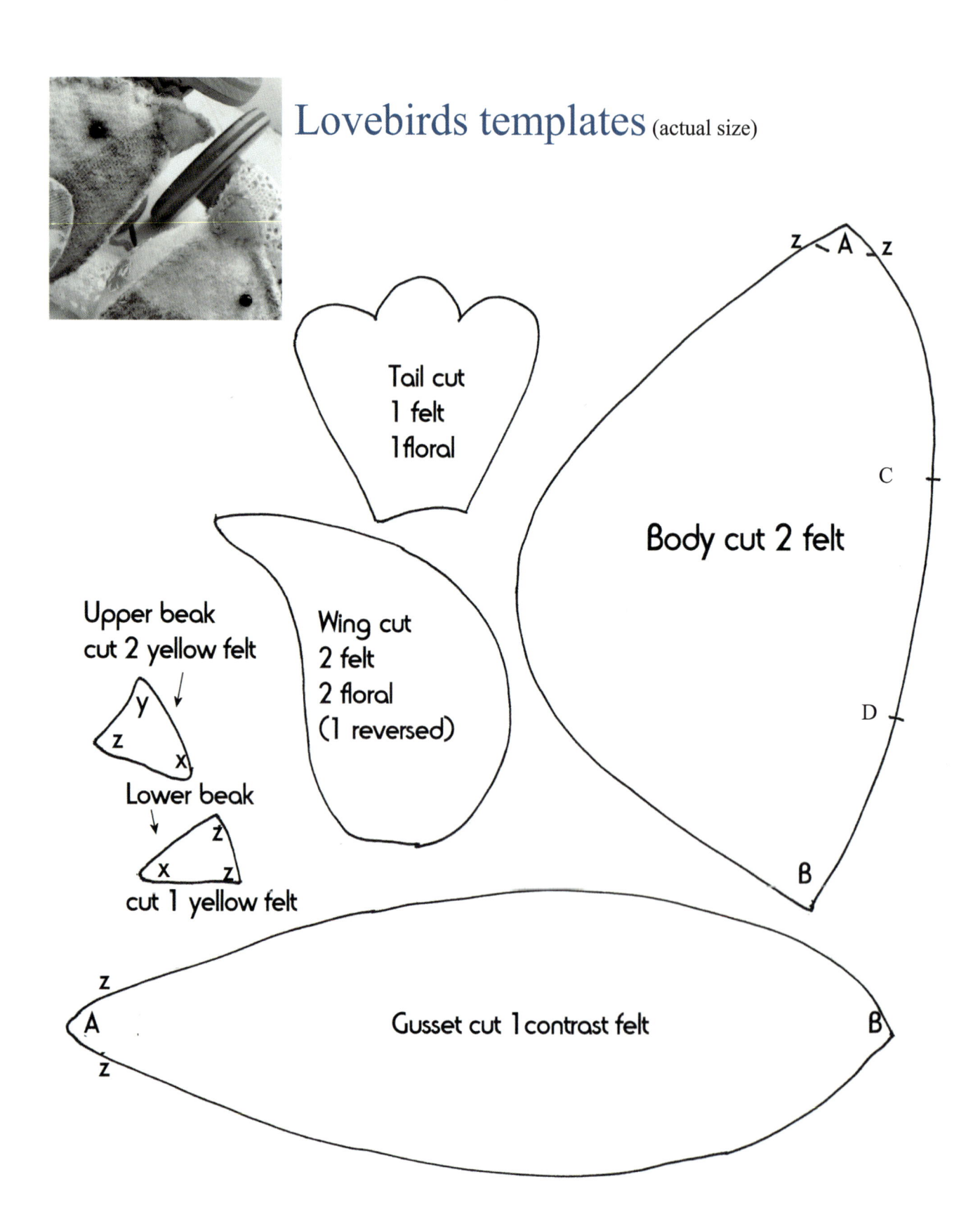

Tail cut
1 felt
1 floral

Body cut 2 felt

Upper beak
cut 2 yellow felt

Wing cut
2 felt
2 floral
(1 reversed)

Lower beak
cut 1 yellow felt

Gusset cut 1 contrast felt

54

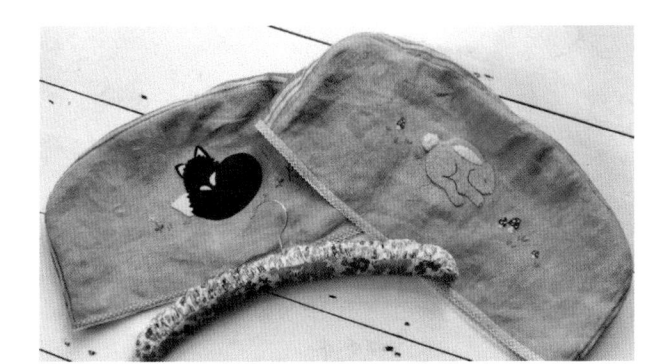

Snuggle Clothes Covers

Templates are actual size and reversed for tracing onto the paper side of your Bondaweb

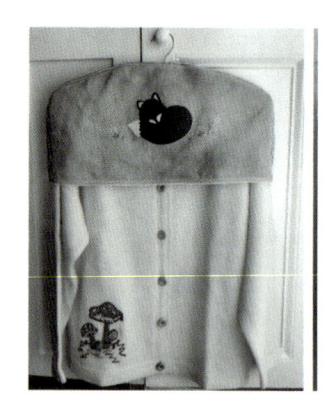

Applique Cardigan

Template is actual size and reversed for tracing onto the paper side of your Bondaweb

Bunny Template

This is the actual size I used for the smallest of my three bunnies in a row. I increased the size by 50% for the larger two bunnies.

I haven't included the templates at larger sizes as this will take up so many pages nd it's quite easy to do on a photocopier or even by using the old fashioned grid method.

This is the actual size of the transfer I used to frame my bunny in a 7" hoop.

Printed in Great Britain
by Amazon.co.uk, Ltd.,
Marston Gate.